EMMANUEL JOSEPH

The Power of Modern Administration Technique For Glory Aquisition

Copyright © 2025 by Emmanuel Joseph

All rights reserved. No part of this publication may be reproduced, stored or transmitted in any form or by any means, electronic, mechanical, photocopying, recording, scanning, or otherwise without written permission from the publisher. It is illegal to copy this book, post it to a website, or distribute it by any other means without permission.

First edition

*This book was professionally typeset on Reedsy.
Find out more at reedsy.com*

Contents

1. Chapter 1: Understanding Modern Administration — 1
2. Chapter 2: The Role of Technology in Modern Administration — 3
3. Chapter 3: Streamlining Processes with Automation — 5
4. Chapter 4: Enhancing Communication and Collaboration — 7
5. Chapter 5: Data Management and Analysis — 9
6. Chapter 6: Project Management Techniques — 11
7. Chapter 7: Financial Management and Budgeting — 13
8. Chapter 8: Human Resources and Talent Management — 15
9. Chapter 9: Regulatory Compliance and Risk Management — 17
10. Chapter 10: Customer Relationship Management — 19
11. Chapter 11: Continuous Improvement and Innovation — 21
12. Chapter 12: The Future of Modern Administration — 23

1

Chapter 1: Understanding Modern Administration

Modern administration is no longer confined to the walls of an office or the limitations of traditional methods. It has evolved into a dynamic and adaptive discipline that harnesses the power of technology, data, and innovative strategies to enhance organizational efficiency and effectiveness. The transformation from antiquated administrative techniques to modern approaches has been driven by the need to keep pace with rapid technological advancements and the ever-changing demands of the global market.

In the realm of modern administration, technology serves as the backbone that supports and streamlines operations. From cloud computing and artificial intelligence to advanced data analytics and automation, technology has revolutionized the way administrative tasks are performed. These innovations have not only made processes more efficient but have also empowered administrators to focus on strategic decision-making and value-added activities, rather than being bogged down by routine tasks.

Furthermore, the role of administrators has shifted significantly. No longer mere facilitators of day-to-day operations, modern administrators are strategic partners who play a crucial role in driving organizational success. They are expected to possess a diverse skill set that includes technological proficiency, data literacy, and a keen understanding of business dynamics. This shift in responsibilities underscores the importance of continuous learning and professional development in the field of administration.

The adoption of modern administration techniques is essential for organizations to remain competitive and agile. In today's fast-paced business environment, the ability to quickly adapt to changes and make informed decisions is paramount. Modern administrative practices enable organizations to respond swiftly to market fluctuations, customer needs, and regulatory requirements, ensuring long-term sustainability and growth.

Ultimately, the power of modern administration lies in its ability to integrate technology, streamline processes, and foster a culture of innovation. By embracing these techniques, organizations can achieve higher levels of productivity, improve communication and collaboration, and create a more agile and resilient workforce. As we delve deeper into the subsequent chapters, we will explore the various facets of modern administration and uncover the strategies and tools that can drive organizational success.

2

Chapter 2: The Role of Technology in Modern Administration

Technology has fundamentally reshaped the landscape of administration, bringing about transformative changes in the way organizations operate. The advent of digital tools and platforms has enabled administrators to enhance productivity, streamline processes, and achieve higher levels of accuracy in their work. In this chapter, we will explore the various ways in which technology plays a pivotal role in modern administration.

One of the most significant advancements in technology is the use of cloud computing. Cloud-based solutions offer administrators the flexibility to access data and applications from anywhere, at any time. This has revolutionized the way administrative tasks are performed, allowing for seamless collaboration and real-time updates. Cloud computing also provides enhanced data security and storage capabilities, ensuring that sensitive information is protected and easily retrievable.

Another key technological innovation is the use of artificial intelligence (AI) and machine learning. These technologies have the potential to automate routine administrative tasks, such as data entry, scheduling, and document management. By leveraging AI-powered tools, administrators can focus on more strategic and value-added activities. Additionally, AI can analyze vast amounts of data to provide valuable insights, helping administrators make informed decisions and drive continuous improvement.

Communication tools have also seen significant advancements, facilitating better collaboration and information sharing. Platforms such as Microsoft Teams, Slack, and Zoom have become integral to modern administration, enabling administrators to communicate with team members, stakeholders, and clients efficiently. These tools support various forms of communication, including instant messaging, video conferencing, and file sharing, making it easier to coordinate efforts and stay connected.

Moreover, technology has transformed data management practices. Advanced data analytics tools allow administrators to collect, organize, and analyze data with precision and accuracy. This enables organizations to identify trends, measure performance, and make data-driven decisions. The integration of data analytics into administrative processes ensures that decisions are based on solid evidence, leading to better outcomes and improved efficiency.

In conclusion, technology is at the heart of modern administration, driving innovation and efficiency. By embracing digital tools and platforms, administrators can enhance their capabilities, streamline processes, and achieve higher levels of productivity. The role of technology in administration is ever-evolving, and staying abreast of the latest advancements is crucial for organizations to remain competitive and agile.

3

Chapter 3: Streamlining Processes with Automation

Automation is a game-changer in modern administration, offering a myriad of benefits that can significantly enhance organizational efficiency. By automating routine and repetitive tasks, administrators can save valuable time and resources, reduce the risk of errors, and focus on more strategic activities. In this chapter, we will delve into the various aspects of process automation and its impact on modern administration.

One of the primary advantages of automation is the ability to streamline workflows. By automating tasks such as data entry, scheduling, and document management, organizations can eliminate bottlenecks and ensure that processes run smoothly. Automation tools can handle these tasks with greater speed and accuracy than manual efforts, leading to increased productivity and efficiency. Furthermore, automated workflows can be easily monitored and adjusted, allowing administrators to optimize processes continually.

Another significant benefit of automation is the reduction of human error. Manual tasks are prone to mistakes, which can lead to costly repercussions for an organization. Automation minimizes the risk of errors by ensuring that tasks are performed consistently and accurately. For instance, automated data entry tools can extract and input data with precision, reducing the likelihood of discrepancies and improving data integrity.

Automation also plays a crucial role in enhancing communication and collaboration within an organization. Tools such as automated email responses, chatbots, and scheduling assistants can facilitate better communication and ensure that tasks are completed on time. These tools can also provide real-time updates and notifications, keeping team members informed and aligned. By automating communication processes, administrators can foster a more cohesive and collaborative work environment.

In addition to streamlining workflows and reducing errors, automation can also lead to significant cost savings. By automating routine tasks, organizations can reduce the need for manual labor and allocate resources more efficiently. This can result in lower operational costs and improved financial performance. Moreover, automation can help identify inefficiencies and areas for improvement, enabling organizations to implement cost-saving measures.

In summary, automation is a powerful tool in modern administration, offering numerous benefits that can enhance efficiency, accuracy, and collaboration. By leveraging automation tools, administrators can streamline processes, reduce errors, and achieve cost savings. Embracing automation is essential for organizations to stay competitive and agile in today's fast-paced business environment.

4

Chapter 4: Enhancing Communication and Collaboration

Effective communication and collaboration are the cornerstones of successful administration. In the modern workplace, administrators must leverage a variety of tools and techniques to ensure that information flows seamlessly and that team members work together harmoniously. In this chapter, we will explore the strategies and technologies that can enhance communication and collaboration in an organization.

One of the most impactful tools for improving communication is the use of collaboration platforms. Software such as Microsoft Teams, Slack, and Asana allows team members to communicate in real-time, share files, and collaborate on projects. These platforms support various forms of communication, including instant messaging, video conferencing, and task management. By centralizing communication and collaboration efforts, these tools help administrators keep everyone on the same page and ensure that projects progress smoothly.

Video conferencing has also become an essential component of modern administration. With the rise of remote work and global teams, video conferencing tools such as Zoom, Google Meet, and Microsoft Teams enable administrators to conduct virtual meetings and maintain face-to-face communication. These tools facilitate real-time discussions, presentations, and brainstorming sessions, making it easier to coordinate efforts and build strong relationships with team members and stakeholders.

Instant messaging is another valuable tool for enhancing communication in an organization. Platforms like Slack and Microsoft Teams provide administrators with the ability to send quick messages, share updates, and seek clarification on tasks. Instant messaging fosters a more responsive and agile work environment, allowing team members to address issues and make decisions promptly. Additionally, these platforms often include features such as chat channels and integrations with other tools, further enhancing their functionality.

To foster a culture of collaboration, administrators must also focus on creating an inclusive and supportive work environment. Encouraging open communication, active listening, and mutual respect can help build trust and strengthen relationships within the team. Administrators can also promote collaboration by recognizing and celebrating team achievements, providing opportunities for professional development, and facilitating team-building activities.

In conclusion, effective communication and collaboration are essential for successful administration. By leveraging collaboration platforms, video conferencing tools, and instant messaging, administrators can enhance communication, streamline workflows, and foster a collaborative culture. Building strong relationships and maintaining open lines of communication are key to achieving organizational success.

5

Chapter 5: Data Management and Analysis

In the era of big data, effective data management and analysis are critical components of modern administration. Administrators must be adept at collecting, organizing, and analyzing data to make informed decisions and drive continuous improvement. In this chapter, we will explore the importance of data management and the tools and techniques available for data analysis.

Data management involves the systematic collection, storage, and organization of data to ensure its accuracy, accessibility, and security. Effective data management practices enable organizations to maintain reliable and up-to-date information, which is essential for decision-making. Administrators must implement robust data management systems that can handle the volume and complexity of data generated by modern businesses. This includes selecting the right software, establishing data governance policies, and ensuring compliance with data protection regulations.

One of the key aspects of data management is data integrity. Administrators must ensure that data is accurate, consistent, and free from errors. This involves implementing data validation techniques, conducting regular audits, and establishing data quality standards. By maintaining high data integrity, organizations can trust the information they use for decision-making and avoid costly mistakes.

Data analysis is the process of examining data to uncover patterns, trends, and insights. Advanced analytics tools enable administrators to analyze large datasets with precision and speed. Techniques such as descriptive analytics, predictive analytics, and prescriptive analytics provide valuable insights that can inform strategic decisions and drive continuous improvement. Administrators must be proficient in using these tools and interpreting the results to make data-driven decisions.

Data visualization is another important aspect of data analysis. Visualization tools such as Tableau, Power BI, and Google Data Studio allow administrators to create interactive and visually appealing dashboards and reports. These tools help convey complex information in a clear and understandable manner, making it easier for stakeholders to grasp key insights. Effective data visualization can enhance communication, support decision-making, and drive organizational success.

In summary, effective data management and analysis are crucial for modern administration. By implementing robust data management practices and leveraging advanced analytics tools, administrators can make informed decisions, identify opportunities for improvement, and drive organizational success. The ability to collect, organize, and analyze data with precision is a valuable skill that modern administrators must possess.

6

Chapter 6: Project Management Techniques

Project management is a fundamental aspect of modern administration, requiring administrators to plan, execute, and oversee projects effectively. Successful project management involves coordinating resources, managing timelines, and ensuring that objectives are met. In this chapter, we will explore the key principles and techniques of project management and how they can be applied to administrative tasks.

One of the core principles of project management is effective planning. Administrators must define clear project goals, establish timelines, and allocate resources to ensure that projects are completed successfully. This involves creating detailed project plans that outline tasks, milestones, and deliverables. Effective planning sets the foundation for project success and helps administrators anticipate potential challenges and risks.

Project management methodologies provide structured approaches to managing projects. Two of the most popular methodologies are Agile and Waterfall. Agile emphasizes iterative development, continuous feedback, and flexibility, making it ideal for projects that require rapid adjustments and collaboration. Waterfall, on the other hand, follows a linear and sequential approach, with each phase of the project dependent on the completion of the previous one. Understanding and selecting the appropriate methodology based on the project's nature and requirements is crucial for administrators.

Resource allocation is another critical aspect of project management. Administrators must ensure that resources such as personnel, budget, and equipment are effectively distributed to meet project objectives. This involves identifying the necessary resources, assigning tasks to team members, and monitoring resource utilization throughout the project. Effective resource allocation helps prevent bottlenecks and ensures that projects stay on track.

Risk management is an integral part of project management. Administrators must identify potential risks, assess their impact, and develop mitigation strategies. This involves conducting risk assessments, creating contingency plans, and regularly monitoring risk factors. By proactively managing risks, administrators can minimize their impact on the project and ensure that objectives are met.

In conclusion, effective project management is essential for successful administration. By implementing robust planning, selecting appropriate methodologies, allocating resources efficiently, and managing risks, administrators can ensure that projects are completed on time and within budget. Mastering project management techniques is a valuable skill that can drive organizational success.

7

Chapter 7: Financial Management and Budgeting

Sound financial management is a cornerstone of modern administration, essential for maintaining organizational stability and achieving long-term success. Administrators play a critical role in managing budgets, tracking expenses, and ensuring financial health. In this chapter, we will explore the principles and practices of financial management and budgeting in modern administration.

Effective budgeting is the foundation of financial management. Administrators must create detailed budgets that outline projected income and expenses for a specific period. This involves identifying funding sources, estimating costs, and allocating funds to various departments and projects. A well-structured budget provides a roadmap for financial planning and helps organizations allocate resources efficiently.

Tracking and monitoring expenses are crucial for maintaining financial health. Administrators must regularly review financial statements, track expenditures, and compare them against the budget. This allows organizations to identify variances, address overspending, and make informed decisions about resource allocation. Effective expense tracking also ensures that funds are used efficiently and that financial goals are met.

Financial forecasting is another essential aspect of financial management.

Administrators must analyze historical data and market trends to predict future financial performance. This involves creating financial models, projecting revenue and expenses, and identifying potential risks and opportunities. Accurate financial forecasting helps organizations plan for the future, make strategic investments, and achieve long-term goals.

Cost-saving strategies are vital for maintaining financial stability. Administrators must identify areas where costs can be reduced without compromising quality or productivity. This involves conducting cost-benefit analyses, negotiating with vendors, and implementing efficiency measures. By adopting cost-saving strategies, organizations can improve their financial performance and ensure sustainable growth.

In summary, effective financial management and budgeting are essential for modern administration. By creating detailed budgets, tracking expenses, forecasting financial performance, and implementing cost-saving strategies, administrators can ensure that organizations achieve financial stability and long-term success. Mastering financial management skills is crucial for administrators to drive organizational growth and stability.

8

Chapter 8: Human Resources and Talent Management

People are the backbone of any organization, and effective human resource management is essential for modern administration. Administrators play a critical role in managing talent, fostering a positive work environment, and ensuring employee satisfaction. In this chapter, we will explore the key principles and practices of human resources and talent management.

Recruitment and onboarding are the first steps in talent management. Administrators must develop strategies to attract and hire the best talent. This involves creating job descriptions, advertising positions, conducting interviews, and selecting candidates. Effective onboarding programs help new employees acclimate to the organization, understand their roles, and become productive members of the team.

Training and development are crucial for employee growth and organizational success. Administrators must identify training needs, design development programs, and provide opportunities for continuous learning. This involves conducting skills assessments, organizing workshops, and offering mentorship programs. By investing in employee development, organizations can enhance their capabilities and achieve long-term goals.

Performance evaluation is an essential aspect of talent management. Administrators must establish performance metrics, conduct regular evaluations, and provide constructive feedback. This helps employees understand their strengths and areas for improvement, set goals, and enhance their performance. Effective performance evaluation also supports career advancement and employee retention.

Fostering a positive work environment is vital for employee satisfaction and productivity. Administrators must create a culture of respect, inclusion, and collaboration. This involves promoting open communication, recognizing and rewarding achievements, and addressing conflicts promptly. A positive work environment enhances employee morale, reduces turnover, and drives organizational success.

In conclusion, effective human resource management and talent management are critical for modern administration. By developing strategies for recruitment, training, performance evaluation, and fostering a positive work environment, administrators can ensure that organizations attract, retain, and develop the best talent. Mastering human resource management skills is essential for administrators to drive organizational success and create a thriving workforce.

9

Chapter 9: Regulatory Compliance and Risk Management

Compliance with regulations and effective risk management are critical aspects of modern administration. Administrators must ensure that organizations adhere to industry regulations and manage risks to protect the organization's interests. In this chapter, we will explore the principles and practices of regulatory compliance and risk management in modern administration.

Regulatory compliance involves adhering to laws, regulations, and industry standards that govern organizational operations. Administrators must stay up-to-date with relevant regulations, implement compliance programs, and conduct regular audits. This involves understanding legal requirements, developing policies and procedures, and providing training to employees. Effective regulatory compliance helps organizations avoid legal issues, penalties, and reputational damage.

Risk management is the process of identifying, assessing, and mitigating risks that could impact organizational objectives. Administrators must conduct risk assessments, develop risk mitigation strategies, and monitor risk factors continuously. This involves identifying potential risks, evaluating their impact, and implementing controls to minimize their effects. Effective risk management helps organizations navigate uncertainties and ensure business continuity.

Creating a robust compliance program is essential for regulatory adherence and risk management. Administrators must develop policies and procedures that align with regulatory requirements and industry best practices. This involves establishing clear guidelines, providing training to employees, and conducting regular compliance audits. A robust compliance program ensures that organizations operate within legal boundaries and maintain high ethical standards.

Administrators must also foster a culture of compliance and risk awareness within the organization. This involves promoting transparency, encouraging ethical behavior, and providing channels for reporting concerns. By fostering a culture of compliance, administrators can ensure that all employees understand their responsibilities and contribute to regulatory adherence and risk management efforts.

In summary, regulatory compliance and risk management are critical for modern administration. By staying up-to-date with regulations, conducting risk assessments, developing robust compliance programs, and fostering a culture of compliance, administrators can protect organizations from legal and operational risks. Mastering regulatory compliance and risk management skills is essential for administrators to ensure organizational success and sustainability.

10

Chapter 10: Customer Relationship Management

Building and maintaining strong relationships with customers is crucial for any organization's success. Effective customer relationship management (CRM) involves understanding customer needs, providing excellent service, and fostering loyalty. In this chapter, we will explore the key principles and practices of CRM in modern administration.

Understanding customer needs is the first step in effective CRM. Administrators must gather and analyze customer data to gain insights into their preferences, behaviors, and expectations. This involves conducting surveys, analyzing feedback, and monitoring customer interactions. By understanding customer needs, organizations can tailor their products and services to meet their expectations and enhance customer satisfaction.

Providing excellent customer service is essential for building strong relationships. Administrators must develop strategies to deliver exceptional service at every touchpoint. This involves training employees, implementing customer service standards, and resolving issues promptly. Excellent customer service enhances customer loyalty and drives positive word-of-mouth referrals.

CRM software is a valuable tool for managing customer relationships.

These platforms provide a centralized database for storing customer information, tracking interactions, and managing communications. Popular CRM tools include Salesforce, HubSpot, and Zoho CRM. By leveraging CRM software, administrators can streamline processes, improve communication, and ensure that customer needs are met consistently.

Fostering customer loyalty is vital for long-term success. Administrators must implement strategies to retain customers and encourage repeat business. This involves creating loyalty programs, offering personalized experiences, and engaging with customers regularly. By fostering loyalty, organizations can build lasting relationships and achieve sustainable growth.

In conclusion, effective customer relationship management is essential for modern administration. By understanding customer needs, providing excellent service, leveraging CRM software, and fostering loyalty, administrators can build strong relationships and drive organizational success. Mastering CRM skills is crucial for administrators to ensure customer satisfaction and achieve long-term growth.

11

Chapter 11: Continuous Improvement and Innovation

Modern administration is about continuous improvement and innovation. Organizations must strive to enhance their processes, products, and services to remain competitive and achieve long-term success. In this chapter, we will explore the principles and practices of continuous improvement and innovation in modern administration.

Continuous improvement involves the ongoing effort to enhance processes, reduce waste, and increase efficiency. Administrators must adopt a mindset of continuous improvement and encourage team members to identify opportunities for enhancement. This involves implementing methodologies such as Lean, Six Sigma, and Kaizen, which provide structured approaches to process improvement. By embracing continuous improvement, organizations can achieve higher levels of productivity and quality.

Innovation is the process of introducing new ideas, products, or services that create value for the organization and its customers. Administrators must foster a culture of innovation by encouraging creativity, experimentation, and risk-taking. This involves creating an environment where employees feel empowered to share their ideas and collaborate on innovative projects. By nurturing a culture of innovation, organizations can stay ahead of the competition and adapt to changing market conditions.

Technology plays a significant role in driving continuous improvement and innovation. Administrators must leverage digital tools and platforms to streamline processes and enhance productivity. This includes using data analytics to identify areas for improvement, implementing automation to reduce manual tasks, and adopting cloud-based solutions for better collaboration. By integrating technology into their operations, organizations can achieve greater efficiency and innovation.

Effective leadership is essential for driving continuous improvement and innovation. Administrators must lead by example, demonstrating a commitment to excellence and encouraging a growth mindset. This involves setting clear goals, providing resources and support, and recognizing and rewarding innovative efforts. Strong leadership fosters a culture of continuous improvement and innovation, motivating employees to strive for excellence.

In conclusion, continuous improvement and innovation are vital for modern administration. By adopting methodologies for process enhancement, fostering a culture of innovation, leveraging technology, and providing strong leadership, administrators can drive organizational success. Mastering continuous improvement and innovation skills is crucial for administrators to ensure long-term growth and competitiveness.

12

Chapter 12: The Future of Modern Administration

The landscape of modern administration is constantly evolving, with emerging technologies and trends shaping the future of the field. In this chapter, we will explore the future trends and developments in modern administration and the skills that administrators will need to succeed.

Emerging technologies such as artificial intelligence, machine learning, and blockchain are set to revolutionize administrative tasks further. AI and machine learning can automate complex processes, provide predictive insights, and enhance decision-making. Blockchain technology offers secure and transparent solutions for data management and transactions. Administrators must stay abreast of these technological advancements and understand how to integrate them into their operations.

The future of modern administration will also see an increased focus on data-driven decision-making. Administrators will need to harness the power of big data and advanced analytics to gain insights and make informed decisions. This involves developing data literacy skills, understanding data analytics tools, and leveraging data to drive continuous improvement. Data-driven decision-making will be a key competency for administrators in the future.

Remote work and flexible work arrangements are trends that are likely to continue shaping modern administration. Administrators will need to adapt to managing remote teams, ensuring effective communication, and maintaining productivity. This involves leveraging collaboration tools, implementing remote work policies, and fostering a culture of trust and accountability. The ability to manage remote teams effectively will be an essential skill for future administrators.

Sustainability and social responsibility will also play a significant role in the future of modern administration. Organizations will need to adopt sustainable practices, reduce their environmental impact, and contribute to social causes. Administrators will be responsible for developing and implementing sustainability initiatives, tracking progress, and ensuring compliance with environmental regulations. A commitment to sustainability will be a critical factor in organizational success.

In conclusion, the future of modern administration will be shaped by emerging technologies, data-driven decision-making, remote work, and sustainability. Administrators must stay ahead of these trends, continuously update their skills, and embrace innovation to drive organizational success. By preparing for the future, administrators can ensure that their organizations remain competitive and resilient in an ever-changing business landscape.

The Power of Modern Administration Technique

Unlock the secrets to transformative organizational success with "The Power of Modern Administration Technique". This comprehensive guide delves into the cutting-edge strategies and technologies reshaping the world of administration. From leveraging the latest advancements in technology to implementing innovative project management methodologies, this book offers valuable insights and practical advice for administrators seeking to elevate their skills and drive efficiency.

Discover how to harness the power of automation to streamline processes, enhance communication and collaboration, and make data-driven decisions. Learn the principles of effective financial management and budgeting, and explore the critical aspects of human resources and talent management. With

CHAPTER 12: THE FUTURE OF MODERN ADMINISTRATION

a focus on regulatory compliance and risk management, this book provides the tools and techniques needed to navigate the complexities of modern administration.

Embrace a culture of continuous improvement and innovation, and stay ahead of future trends with insights into emerging technologies and remote work strategies. Whether you're a seasoned administrator or just starting your career, "The Power of Modern Administration Technique" equips you with the knowledge and skills to thrive in today's dynamic business environment.

Join the ranks of forward-thinking administrators who are revolutionizing their organizations with modern techniques. This book is your essential guide to mastering the art of administration and achieving long-term success.

www.ingramcontent.com/pod-product-compliance
Lightning Source LLC
LaVergne TN
LVHW010445070526
838199LV00066B/6207